LIFE'S
EXPERIENCES

Glenda Hummel,
You have changed so
many lives and you
don't even get any
acknowledge but I
do remember!

LIFE'S
EXPERIENCES
Truth, Honesty, Hatred, And Love

PAUL HER

To order additional copies of this book, contact:
Xlibris Corporation
1-888-795-4274
www.Xlibris.com
Orders@Xlibris.com
130298

Contents

Breathless 11

Trayvon Martin 12

Lansing, Michigan..13

Life Is 14

Hard Times 15

I Promise 16

Amazed 17

It Is True..18

I Vow 19

As 20

Without You 21

My Questions? 22

Believe...23

Your Love...24

Inside Me 25

Solemnly Swear 26

I Would (Never Win Her) 27

Long Gone..28

My Thoughts 29

The Truth...30

Understanding 31

Meant To Be...32

Fate 33

Game 34

Anything...35

You Are More..36

...nt 37

...eart 38

...mer 39

...nique 40

You Are 41

What Is a Love Touch? 42

Take My Hands 43

I Was Stunned 44

When I First Met You 45

What Is Honesty? 46

You Are Unique 47

True Beauty 48

First Love 50

I Hope 51

Nature 52

The Will To Win 53

Tough 54

Will Be There 55

I Still 56

You 57

An Inspiration 58

A Hmong Girl 60

Sister 61

Magic Johnson 62

Wash Me Away 63

Friendship 64

Cry 65

Be Something 66

Be Humble 67

My Words 68

I'm Sorry 69

Honey 70

Dedication

I would like to dedicate this book to my sisters, Mai Xiong Her and Mai Doua Her. I want them to know that no matter what, I will always love them. Life is full of pain and struggles, but we have to understand that in time, it gets better. I wrote this book thinking of them and how their lives have turned out. Although, they have seen ups and downs, I am proud of the poise they have displayed. Life is a mere memory of events that one will experience. With that said, live your life for the moments that take your breath away.

Acknowledgement

I would like to first acknowledge my uncle, Lor Her, for being my other father figure, as I was a teenager. Your love and care will not go unnoticed until the end of time. Thank you for all you have done for me from the Vipers Soccer Era, and throughout my college years. My second acknowledgement is for my uncle, Xue Her, who is truly one of my best friends. He is the reason for me becoming a poet. We spent many hours reading hallmark cards to find the perfect words to express to his girlfriend (Now his wife). Wonderful days!!!

Breathless

The reflection of your shadow
Left a shade in my heart

The smell of your natural scent
Left a fume of lasting rosy smell

The smile on your face
Left a feeling of satisfaction on my mind

The sound of your words
Left a sensational harmony through my ears

The love of your heart
Left a breathless memory in my life

Trayvon Martin

He was born to a world where racism shouldn't exist
He lived in a state where discrimination is not accepted
Trayvon Martin was his name and he will be missed
A young man with a dream
Got killed and was only a teen
A nation disrupted by anger
His fellow citizens left with questions unanswered?
We will never know the truth
Even with all the speculations, facts, and clues
All we can do is find justice
March, protest, rally, and try our best
Surely, race played an important part
Let this be a lesson, all people should look into their hearts
Please don't blame the sweatshirt hoodie
Just let Trayvon Martin lie in peace and dignity

Lansing, Michigan

No matter where I may end up
There's always this special place in my heart

A place that I will always belong
And to me, it will always be home

This is not the greatest place on earth
But it's the place of my soul's birth

This place shaped the person I am
And made me into a man

I will never forget the wonderful memories
And the white beautiful winter sceneries

Although it will be a long time before I go back
My friends and family there are still the best

I know one day I will live there again
In this beautiful place, call Lansing, Michigan

Life Is . . .

Life is a wonderful thing
Life is precious
Life is beautiful
Life is what you live
Life is devastating
Life is filled with sorrows
Life is full of joy
Life is love
Life is pain
Life is learning
Life is exciting
And most important, life is you

Hard Times

I pretended there was no pain in the midst of your affairs
Staying in denial because I was scared
I didn't want to face the truth
In a world I know I'm bound to lose
There were moments where my heart stopped
And all my dignity dropped
In my mind I didn't think I was going to survive
But today I cannot be happier that I'm alive
In this process I have seen the dark side
And in this life I have found many lies
But none of them hurt as much as yours
Because in reality only you could give me more
With a million words spoken, only yours get to my heart
Why didn't you think before you took us apart?
In the struggles of hard times
You ran to someone else and left me behind

I Promise

For you I promise forever
Always to be together
Not only in this lifetime
But through eternity
For you I promise reality
Only honesty
And protected security
For you I promise my heart
Never to be apart
Any second, any minute, any hour, or any day
For you I promise trust
Just love, no lust
Only for you will I promise all this.

Amazed

Talking to you was so amazing
The sound of your voice was very sweet
The memories of our conversation just started phasing
And every time I think about it, my heart skips a beat

I'm longing for a glimpse of your pretty face
Because last night I couldn't fall asleep
Everything you told me left me amazed
And I can now appreciate your love for life because it is deep

The way you are, you bring me so much grace
I hope in this lifetime you can be mine to reach
But if I can't have you, our short story will be embraced
Because in my life, you will never be erased

It Is True

It is true that in this millennium
My parents cannot read or write
They cannot even speak English properly

It is true that my people
The Hmong people did not even have a writing system
Until the early 1950's

It is true that most Hmong children
Have to achieve academics without any guidance
Due to the lack of education of our parents.

It is true that the Hmong is without a country
But they've found peace and tranquility
In every region to which they've migrated

It is true that we are one of the smallest groups of minority
In the United States of America
But this doesn't mean our opportunities are limited

It is true that we can achieve greatness in America
Because with freedom, justice and little discrimination
We are using our abilities to reach the platform of success

I Vow . . .

I vow . . .

To love and cherish you through thick and thin
To obey and respect you
To suffer through harsh times
To serve as your heart desires
To be honest and caring
To protect you from any harm
To guide you through life
To be your soul mate
To be your partner in heaven
To stay with you forever
To always be there for you

As bright as the sun
That's the glow of your face

As dark as the night
That's the secret of your life

As heartless as a hungry lion
That's the heart of yours

As ruthless as a pack of hyenas
That's the traits you possess

As cold as the freezing winter
That's the blood in your veins

As lonely as the empty forest
That's the life you will get

Without You

If I were to live forever I wouldn't choose
Because in life we are born to lose
And I don't want to live a life without you
Because when you are gone
I'll be lost without a clue
Living alone without half of my heart
Is like living only in the dark
When I'm a puzzle with a missing piece
I can never be a complete masterpiece
And it doesn't matter if I am a success
Without you, my will to live wouldn't last
If I were to die with you, I'll choose
Because I would rather spend eternity lying next to you

My Questions?

Will life be the same without you?
Will the sky still be blue?
Can I survive through the long nights?
Can I win against the fights?

Will love be the same if not for you?
Will the ocean water still be blue?
Can I breathe without your heart?
Can I win when we are apart?

Will food still taste the same when you are gone?
Without you, can the world be wrong?
Can I find the will to laugh?
Can I invent a time machine to get back to the past?

Believe

Let me tell you this
If you just make a wish
I could make it come true
Just believe, I'll never hurt you
As a promise, I will always be true
And if your sky is black
I'll turn it back to blue
Please believe that I will always care
And whenever you need me, I'll be there
Day by day I will make you see
That my feelings are real
So all you have to do is believe

Your Love

Your love is like the wind of a twister
Swirling through my heart like a disaster
Always breaking me into pieces
And leaving me behind like I'm some kind of disease

Your careless heart is like an erupting volcano
Burning me into ashes with no sorrows
Leaving me to suffocate in this polluted air
Hopeless, lost, alone, and scared

Your promiscuous personality is like the storms of hurricanes
Heading in every direction that will satisfied your cravings
Never realizing that my heart is broken
And soon the door to my love will be closing

Inside Me

Despite all the glamour
Away from the fame
Like you, I am a lonely human being

Take away all my money
Remove all my fancy cars
Inside me, there are many unhealed scars

Destroy my bigger-than-life image
Erase the name I've built
Like yours, my heart can melt

Shut off all the cameras
Leave behind my popular reputation
Inside me, you and I are the same

Solemnly Swear

As I stand here to solemnly swear
That for you I'll always be there
The little things you do to make me smile
Will always carry my love across the miles
For me, one little kiss of yours
Will be worth more than a million whores
As I come here to give you my heart
In return all I need is for you to play your part
I don't need anything from you
Because your gift to me is you being yourself
As for me, I'll never take you for granted
Because I understand that your love cannot be rented

I Would (Never Win Her)

I thought about it and I didn't want anyone to know
I tried to be strong and not let it show
To arrive at this conclusion it wasn't easy
Thinking about the truth still makes me dizzy

I had to write it down in order for people to understand
That one could only find peace if he could be a truthful man
I have to admit it was hard letting you go
In this instance my whole world was moving very slow

I knew I couldn't have you but I refused to give up
Because in you I believe I could find true love
Again I was too naïve to see
That your tremendous beauty was too much for me

And in this lifetime I know I couldn't satisfy you
No matter how hard I'll try, I would never win you
Because you're the type of girl who likes to test the water
And as you grow older, your heart will keep growing colder

Long Gone

I know we should part ways
But in our hearts, we hope for one more day
I'm trying to make this work
But every time we talk, it hurts
We have nothing to say to each other
No love, no laughs, and no colors
Only a word here and there
And we both don't seem to care
We should just let it go
Just be honest and let each other know
Even if we stay together
This is not going to last forever
The love we had, has sailed away
And the bad memories are here to stay
Our passion for one another is long gone
So sorry to say, but we don't belong
Being together shouldn't be this rough
Every day it seems to get more and more tough
I don't know about you, but our time is up
So goodbye, today, I am giving up

My Thoughts

Will you choose me if I am one of your choices?
Can you single me out among a thousand voices?

If I ask you to run away . . .
Will you pack up and leave with me today?

If I tell you I'll love you till the end of time . . .
Will you open your heart for mine?

Can you be my girl if I ask you?
Will your heart always be true?

If I open my heart for yours . . .
Will you keep loving me more?

If I tell you I'll always adore you . . .
Will you tell me the same thing too?

The Truth

Learn to accept life for what it is
Attachment will only make you fall deep
Accept with full responsibility
Of life's experiences as it is given to you

Because in each experience
There is a lesson to be learned
And within each lesson, we can all grow
As we grow, we learn to appreciate life

With great appreciation and more enlightenment
We can improve the quality of our lives
As we make improvements, we will realize
That the truth is found in all honesty

Understanding

I don't know why we keep on fighting
Talking about issues that can never come to an understanding
Why do you always have to be reassured?
When you yourself are not completely pure
Just believe in the words I say
And we won't have to argue every single day
I am tired of giving you the same answers
And nothing ever changes afterwards
We come across the same issues day in and day out
Sometimes I don't even know what the arguments are about?
I don't know why you can never understand
When everyday I try to become a changed man
I always do my best to impress you
But I guess the message is not coming through
Just give me a true understanding
So I can get this relationship on the road to winning

Meant To Be

She told me it was terrible what she did
In her heart, she is sorry with a deep apology
She has asked for my forgiveness
And I told her, she has been forgiven
Life happened the way it did
Because it's supposed to be that way
For her, I have no hatred
Nor, do I have regrets
I still love her for the person I once knew
Maybe, I'll always love her
Although she has changed
She has blossomed into the person
She is meant to be
In life, we cannot hide our identity
We'd rather be criticized for the truth
Than praised for living a lie
Happiness is living life the way one wants
And it doesn't matter what the sacrifice is
We have to face the consequences
For the choices we have taken
So for her, I've understood
Why she has done what she did
I have been hurt, but from this experience
My life will flourish into true happiness

Fate

I've always believed in you and me
As far as I have gone
You are the only girl I see
Fate is always our destiny
And I know that one day we will be

As much as we have drifted apart
You are always kept in my heart
Fate has a reason
And with you, my life has no seasons
As long as I live
For you, everything I'll try to give

But in the end
If I can't win your heart
Then I'll settle to be your best friend
Even though we're far apart

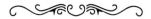

Game

At the time we met, I didn't know
It was just going be fun and games
That quickly you would let me go
Leaving me behind with lots of pain

I didn't see it in you
To break my heart into pieces
Because your words sounded so true
I also believed in your kisses

Your venom was lethal beyond belief
Causing me to fall deep into your trap
I suppose you don't have any grief
Because your heart is as filthy as crap

If I had known you were using me
I would have shown you my kind of game
And let you see
How bad it is to feel the pain

Anything

Nothing compares to the sound of your voice
Everything about you is exciting
Even your writings still quench the smallest nerves in my body
If I could see you for one second
It would last me for a thousand years
The image of your face would never disappear
Because your elegance is everlasting
And your presence is all a blessing
To me, to the world, and to the universe
To this earth, you are worth everything
And in fairness, for you, I'll do anything

You Are More

As the light shines upon you
You are more beautiful than
The glow of a flawless diamond

As the sun reflects upon your face
You are more stunning than
The view of a priceless gallery

As the moon casts upon you
You are more amazing than
The sunrise of a breathless morning

As the brightest star twinkles upon you
You are more gorgeous than
The princess of any kingdom

A Moment

In a moment of mesmerizing
It's your beauty that captures my eyes
In this breath-taking moment
My heart stops for the scent of your smell
Trying to live this moment forever
Where two unimaginable paths have crossed
In reality I have no chance
But in this fantasy I am the creator
The one who will win this beautiful creature
Whom God himself cannot believe
Such a beauty could be created among human beings

My Heart

You hold the key to my heart
Only you can unlock the forbidden mystery inside of me
You know you have had my heart from the start
Only you can interpret the things I see

Without you, I cannot function correctly
And my hopes and dreams are fading slowly
Inside of me, my heart is dying quietly
Please give me a sign that you still love me

Just show one gesture that you still care for me
Time will not help; it will only make my heart bleed
Put aside your stubbornness
And show me you still want us to be

Summer

Before we know it
The summer will be over
Just fall and I'll catch you
You can just lie on my shoulders
For once let's make this summer last forever
Put your trust in me
We will always be together
Because in my eyes
We are the perfect lovers
Cherish this moment and hold on
Because once she is gone
She is gone forever
They say once in a blue moon
There comes one like no others
Since I have found you
Let's make this season
An everlasting summer

Unique

You requested to receive a poem
I don't know you much
But I'll try to be brief in this form
I see that in your heart
You are nice and pure
And to your friends, you play a special part
Because in each one of them you deeply care
Your passion for friendships is unique
Whenever someone needs anything, you'll always be there
So remember that without you, no one is complete
And that everyone you know loves you with care
Because you are very special and superbly unique

You Are . . .

You are my world, without you, it means nothing to me
You are the light that shines in my path
You complete me; you comfort me, and warm my soul
You are my eyes and my ears
Without you, I am worthless

You are my goddess
You are worth far more than the world itself
You are my sunshine after the rain
You are my happiness and my laughter
Without you, I'd rather not live

You are yourself and that means more than gold
Your smile brightens up my day
You are my strength, my hope, and my love
You are mine and I am the luckiest man alive
Without you, the world is a blind place

What Is a Love Touch?

A Love Touch is . . .

A touch that heats up your body
A touch that boils the blood in your veins
A touch that comforts you completely
A touch that shelters you from the storm
A touch that makes you feel an adrenaline rush from head to toe
A touch that sends love throughout your being
A touch that says I love you and I will protect you
A touch that warms your heart for endless days
A touch like yours

Take My Hands

I know you have been hurt in the past
And I understand that nothing is meant to last
But let me show you my love
A complete feeling that only comes from above

I'm here to stay
And I'll promise to take your breath away
I'll do anything to show you that I care
Because for any reason I'll always be there

If you don't trust me
Every day I will try to make you see
All I want to be is your superman
And all you have to be is my wonder woman

For you I will move mountains apart
And will not stop until I win your heart
Even if you don't believe in love again
I want you to trust me and take my hands

I Was Stunned

I saw this gorgeous girl
And I couldn't take my eyes off her
I tried to control my feelings
But my mind was out of this world
And though I tried to change my view
My eyes just kept wandering back to her
I tried to talk to her but no words came out
I was stunned
And when I saw her staring at me
I thought my heart was going to burst
I knew I wanted her name
But my nerves just kept trembling
So after I left
I noticed from that moment on
Nothing is ever the same
Because I was stunned
That someone like her is a human being

When I First Met You

When I first met you
My sky turned blue
My whole life sparkled
When I first met you
I knew I would love you
Since then my soul has deepened
Since I first met you
I have lied for you
Because I know our love is true

What Is Honesty?

Honesty is being true to yourself
Honesty is trust
Honesty is love
Honesty is being true to your heart
Honesty is friendship
Honesty is leadership
Honesty is being true to your soul
Honesty is power
Honesty is respect
Honesty is being true to your body
Honesty is peace
Honesty is honor
And honesty is what you represent

You Are Unique

You are unique in each and every way
I wish to see your pretty face everyday

The way you are
You make me want to reach for the stars

Your character is so flawless
And your smile can make any man feel breathless

No matter what people say about you
Your pure heart will always be true

You are superbly unique
Because to me, you are as a priceless antique

True Beauty

True Beauty . . .

    Is beauty that everyone memorizes forever
    Is beauty that captures all eyes
    Is beauty that brings smiles upon all
    Is beauty that pumps up the heart 10,000 times faster
    Is beauty that is beyond a goddess
    It beauty that captures all features
    Is beauty that all will die for
    Is beauty that you possess

First Love

I miss the times we used to laugh together
And forever was always on our minds
Whenever we were together
There was never enough time

Although we are apart
You are always
Kept in a special place inside my heart
In my life you will always be in my memories

We were each other's first love
And since the breakup, it has been tough
But time will heal the wound
And we both will find happiness soon

I Hope

When I stand alone
I hope you will be there where I am
When I feel lonely
I hope you will comfort me with your voice

When the world turns against me
I hope you will stand by my side
When no one believes in my abilities
I hope you will give me the inspiration to carry on

When I cannot find the light at the end of the tunnel
I hope you will be my eyes to see
When I can no longer fight for my freedom
I hope you will bring me peace

Nature

The beauty of nature
Lies in the eyes of the beholders
The truth is in the simplicity
And the originality of its form
We cannot deny the offspring of nature
For nature is the giver of lives
As well as the creator of lives
We should not take for granted
The existence of nature
Because extinction is inevitable
And history can repeat itself
For what it is worth, nature must be preserved
As well as reserved for the children of the future
They deserve the natural beauty of nature
As much as the clean oxygen it produces
Without the life of nature, we will lose
Be aware, the decisions we choose
It can affect the outcome of nature
And it can ruin this great world for the future

The Will To Win

Never give up until the final buzzer
Never put the blame on the others
Take the responsibility for your own effort
Always remember what you are after

The will to win is in your heart
If you want to be a winner you have to practice hard
There's no easy way around winning
The only option is to keep on training

Everyday you have to practice twice as much
And although, sometimes winning needs a little bit of luck
You still have to be the best
And you should never want to settle for last

The will to win is in your hands
Because with the right game plans
You can conquer anything your heart desires
Believe in yourself and you will always be a winner

Tough

I adore your unique face in many ways
I believe your beautiful smile should be put in a showcase
Even your eyes are as beautiful as ever
And I know every guy will remember that face forever
Please smile every time I ask you
'Cause you are the only one who could smile so true
I understand that times may be tough
And your situation is rough
But I know that your heart will be strong enough to survive
Because you are a tough person inside
So put away all your sadness
And leave behind your madness
Put a smile upon your face
And all your pain will be erased

Will Be There

When your life was turned upside down
And you couldn't find your way around
She was there to lend you a hand
When you messed up
And no one seems to show you any love
She has always been a friend
When the world turned against you
And no one cared about you
She was there to help you stand tall

Although she is no longer here with us
We know that we will never forget her love
Because she is staring down at us from above

Although you are lonely and sad
Always remember that you are not alone
And that in this world, everything is not all bad
If you cannot withstand the pain
Always know that we care
And whenever you need a hug
We will be there

I Still

It's been so long since I have seen your face
And no, the memories of you have not been erased
I still think about you every single day
Maybe until the day I can no longer breathe

In my eyes you are still the Goddess of beauty
But time has changed my feelings
And it's not by choice
It's by the cards that life is dealing

And yes, I still miss you
But now there's nothing I could do
I have no regrets for this life
Because one day you will make someone a great wife

I know life is not the same without you
But I have to move on, yes I need to
I'm glad that I loved you truly
Because experiencing you made a better man out of me

You

As I sit here staring at you
I can't believe this moment to be true
Your face is far too beautiful
And you are so incredible

The way you make me feel
It is beyond real
Your smile makes me weak
And I feel the butterflies each time you speak

If this is not heaven
Then you must be an angel on earth
To God I am thankful for your birth
And I am pleased with his amazing work

An Inspiration

It seems like we have forgotten about you
But in my heart, I will never let go of you
Time has passed by without a word
It's because the wound still hurts
You know it will never go away
The thought of your graceful face will never fade
Brother, you are an inspiration to me
Even though you are gone, and it killed a part of me
I had to stay strong for the family
And live life with your everlasting memories
I cannot believe it's been over ten years
Life is heartless, I'm so scared
But with you watching over me
My life is full of hope and harmony

A Hmong Girl

The way she makes me feel is unreal
Her black silky hair gives off the best smell

Her average five foot frame
Makes Hmong men go insane

Every time she walks by me
I can't help myself, but I let her be

Her attitude and her beauty give such grace
And especially those dimples on her face

Her yellow skin is so smooth
That every time she touches me I'll lose

Her warm gentle kisses touch my soul
Even in ways that I have never known

This is the sensational feeling of being with her
The perfect beautiful Hmong girl

This is the gift of finding her
The present of receiving a pretty Hmong girl

Sister

No other person can replace my mother
But in you, I believe you could sister

In life, there are not many who can comfort a child
Only a sister who has been a mother for a while

My sister, you are my moon that shines at night
You are my sun that brings me light

Even through all those many fights
Whenever I was down, you've found a way to make everything right

When you have a sister, she is a part of your heart
And with loneliness lingering over you, she'll never part

Without you sister, I'd be lost in my pursuit
In return, I want you to know I love you

Magic Johnson

A boy who had a dream
A teen that had a game
A man who knew how to win
Magic Johnson is his given name

A basketball player from Lansing, Michigan
A champion, who flourished again and again
A father, a role model, a brother, and a great man
A person with HIV, but still stands

A gentleman with a heart of a king
A true leader within his team
A great businessman among his peers
A royal highness to his heir

An innovator who has affected the communities
A guy that has impacted the inner cities
A kind man who made his own fame
Magic Johnson is his given name

Wash Me Away

Can I just wash me away?
Wash my sin, my pain, and my heart
There's so much wrong I have done
Can I earn your support with love?

I am ashamed to not stand by your side
Sometimes, I am afraid of the public perception
I know I should stand for justice
And be firm on my stance against wrongful actions

Can I just wash me away?
Apart from this corruptive world of hatred
Away from the agony of deceitful government bureaucracy
Can I redeem my soul and still be a loyal patriot?

I am confused by the morality of society
By the dishonesty of the many leaders
I know there are still a few decent people left
And I hope we can all unite together for a better future

Friendship

To live and encounter a true friendship
Is a life worth living.

To love and respect a great friendship
Is a gift worth giving.

To care and admire a special friendship
Is a love worth teaching.

To comfort and adore a loyal friendship
Is a feeling worth displaying.

To enjoy and embrace a strong friendship
Is a relationship worth building.

Cry

With life as beautiful, I am so hurt to hear
That the person of you will no longer be here
With sadness I cannot explain
Even with the harmony of heaven, my heart cannot sing

I am heartbroken without you here with us
How can your family survive without your love?
You were the backbone of your household
I thought we were all supposed to live until we are old

I still cannot believe this is true
The tragic news I heard of you
Uncle, there's nothing I can do
All I'm going to do is cry my tears for you

Your time here with us was special
It is going to be hard to let you go
But life happens the way it's supposed to be
So one day, one day, togetherness we will see

Be Something

If I could be something I would be
The wind that brushes against your face

If I could be something I would be
The air that carries the scent of your smell

If I could be something I would be
The mirror that reflects the image of your beauty

If I could be something I would be
The sweat that runs down your body

If I could be something I would be
The song that sings from your lips

If I could be something I would be
The sound that rings sweetly from your laughter

Be Humble

Don't do something because you want approval and attention
Don't climb a mountain because you want to be seen
Don't do a favor because you want the favor back
Don't love because you are expecting love in return

Be humble, do it because you love to do it
Do it because it is the right thing to do

Don't give because it makes you feel good about yourself
Don't fly a plane because you want to be higher than everyone else
Don't speak because you want to hear your own voice
Don't lie because you want to better yourself

Be humble, perform an act for the good of the world
Pay it forward because the world needs an honest good deed

Don't pretend because you want to fit in with others
Don't travel the world because you want to show you are more superior
Don't accept because you are afraid of being different
Don't dream because you want to create a false reality

Be humble, live the truth because you will have no regret
Live the truth because the truth will set you free

My Words

It is hard to find love
I cannot imagine life without it
But if I have to be alone
At least I have tried
I have no regrets
Because I have loved with all my heart
I have been in love
And I have had my first love
I have loved again and again
I am fortunate
But very unlucky at the same time
Maybe I'm cursed
Maybe it's meant to be
But I have had my share of beautiful women
And I have tasted their sweet kisses
At the end I'm still all by myself
I'll be looking for "Her"
This time I'll be wiser
I do want a good wife
In this world it is hard to find a genuine person
Hopefully I will find someone special
And spend the rest of my life with her

I'm Sorry

I' m sorry for calling you names
And ripping all of your pictures from my photo frames
I'm sorry for breaking the window of your car
But I was just trying to cure my broken-heart
I'm sorry for calling you so late
All I wanted to do was to display my hate
I'm sorry for fighting your new man
But it was a request from my friends
I'm sorry for yelling so much at you
At the time, I did want to hurt you
I'm sorry, I'm sorry, but now I'm through with you

Honey

It was by chance, but not by choice
The two of us brought together by a voice
Living in two separate worlds
Leading our lives with different morals

I can say that we are destined to be
And although, our future is never guaranteed
Those two nights we had were indescribable
I have concluded that it was magical

No one has to approve of us
Because in time, we'll show them with our love
Honey, just embrace me with pride
Just believe, this will be one incredible ride

Edwards Brothers Malloy
Thorofare, NJ USA
October 30, 2014